RABBITS
KW-021

Contents

Photography: Dr. Herbert R. Axelrod, Bruce Crook, Marion Cummings, Michael Gilroy, R. Hanson, Burkhard Kahl, D. Robinson, Vincent Serbin, Louise van der Meid.

Title Page: Lop Rabbit. Photo by Bruce Crook.

Distributed in the UNITED STATES by T.F.H. Publications, Inc., One T.F.H. Plaza, Neptune City, NJ 07753; in CANADA to the Pet Trade by H & L Pet Supplies Inc., 27 Kingston Crescent, Kitchener, Ontario N2B 2T6; Rolf C. Hagen Ltd., 3225 Sartelon Street, Montreal 382 Quebec; in CANADA to the Book Trade by Macmillan of Canada (A Division of Canada Publishing Corporation), 164 Commander Boulevard, Agincourt, Ontario M1S 3C7; in ENGLAND by T.F.H. Publications Limited, Cliveden House/Priors Way/Bray, Maidenhead, Berkshire SL6 2HP, England; in AUSTRALIA AND THE SOUTH PACIFIC by T.F.H. (Australia) Pty. Ltd., Box 149, Brookvale 2100 N.S.W., Australia; in NEW ZEALAND by Ross Haines & Son, Ltd., 18 Monmouth Street, Grey Lynn, Auckland 2, New Zealand; in SINGAPORE AND MALAYSIA by MPH Distributors (S) Pte., Ltd., 601 Sims Drive, #03/07/21, Singapore 1438; in the PHILIPPINES by Bio-Research, 5 Lippay Street, San Lorenzo Village, Makati Rizal; in SOUTH AFRICA by Multipet Pty. Ltd., 30 Turners Avenue, Durban 4001. Published by T.F.H. Publications, Inc. Manufactured in the United States of America by T.F.H. Publications, Inc.

RABBITS

EDITED BY PAUL PARADISE

The pleasing color pattern on this rabbit resulted from a cross between white ermine and marten colored rabbits.

True wild rabbits and other small mammals, unlike these specially bred gray rabbits, have a grizzled color pattern called agouti.

Introduction

Classification

Rabbits are mammals, which means that among the most important of the characteristics that distinguish them from other vertebrate animals is the fact that they nourish their young with milk and are in the main covered with hair. There are other big differences between

mammals on the one hand and other backboned animals such as reptiles and amphibians and birds, but those two features are enough to separate rabbits from non-mammals, so we'll stop right there. It's enough to confirm for you what you know already; that rabbits have a lot more in common with you than they have in common with a rattlesnake—which in turn should let you know that you're probably more in tune with the feelings of a pet rabbit than you would be with the feelings of, let's say, a pet frog. You're a mammal, and so is a rabbit.

There are many different mammals, some very strange ones among them. Rabbits belong to one sub-group of animals that share the mammalian characteristics. This sub-group, called the order Lagomorpha, includes rabbits and look-alike animals (the hares and pikas) and is differentiated from other orders of mammals on the basis of certain morphological characteristics, differences in external and internal structures. A rabbit, for example, obviously is not a wolf, yet it is closer in physical makeup to a wolf than it is to, for example, a kangaroo or a bat, both of which, like the wolf, are also mammals but are placed in different orders from the lagomorphs.

The order Lagomorpha is subdivided into two different families, the Ochotonidae (the pikas) and the Leporidae (the hares and rabbits). The family Ochotonidae contains one genus, *Ochotona,* which has about fifteen different species. The pikas look like small brown rabbits; they have much smaller ears than rabbits and have no external tail. They are not kept as pets. The family Leporidae contains eight genera, including the genus *Oryctolagus,* which

A black Dutch rabbit. All domesticated rabbit breeds descended from the European wild rabbit, Oryctolagus cuniculus.

is the genus that we're interested in. We're interested in *Oryctolagus* because its one species is *Oryctolagus cuniculus,* the wild European rabbit, from which all domestic rabbits have descended. All domestic rabbits, regardless of breed or color or size, belong to one species, *O. cuniculus.*

Rabbits have often been confused in popular terminology with another group of lagomorphs, the hares. Strictly speaking, the terms arose so as to

Uniform progeny is the objective of most commercial breeders. This quality is most important in rabbits to be used for medical research.

Opposite: *Cuddly and appealing, rabbits have a distinct charm that makes them attractive as pets to people of all ages, but they are special favorites of children. Today the keeping of rabbits is more popular than ever before, and no doubt the rabbit fancy will grow even more as the pet-seeking public learns more about the advantages rabbits offer.*

allow the differentiation of two similar but distinct European animals, the European wild rabbit (*Oryctolagus*) and *Lepus europeaus,* another wild European lagomorph. The differences between hares and rabbits are not worth worrying about unless you're a taxonomist, because the main difference between hares and rabbits as far as rabbit breeders are concerned is that hares don't lend themselves to domestication anywhere nearly as well as rabbits do. There are of course morphological differences between hares and rabbits, and there are behavioral differences as well. Just keep in mind that the words "rabbit" and "hare" have been thrown around much more loosely than they were intended to be and that the words now are not very reliable as determinants of whether a lagomorph is a true rabbit or a true hare when they

form part of the common name of a lagomorph. The Belgian Hare, for example, one of the domesticated rabbit breeds, is a rabbit, not a hare, and jackrabbits and snowshoe rabbits are not rabbits, they're hares.

So rabbits and hares and pikas are all lagomorphs. They are **not** rodents. They used to be considered to be rodents—and indeed they share with the rodents some common features, ever-growing teeth being one of them—but for many years now most taxonomists have thought them to be sufficiently different from the rodents (order Rodentia) to have their own order.

Commercial Keeping of Rabbits

Rabbits are very important for food, research and fur. Their breeding capacity makes them very valuable and easy to keep. In the United States, the Ozark region, the area of

Although rabbits used to be considered rodents, taxonomists now recognize their differences and have given them a separate order.

northern Arkansas and southern Missouri, is the center for commercial raising of rabbits. It is estimated that the total production for the U.S.A. a year is about 35 million pounds. Rabbits are also important for research, and approximately 2 million are used a year for this purpose.

The world's largest producers and consumers of rabbits are Europeans. This is due to the fact that there is less grazing land available in Europe, making rabbit-keeping much more economically worthwhile than cattle grazing. For the commercial breeder, one doe can be expected to

A Silver Fox rabbit. Silvering is caused by the presence of white-tipped hair distributed evenly throughout the body.

Opposite, top: A Castor Rex rabbit. **Opposite, bottom:** A Harlequin Rex rabbit. This breed is sometimes called the Japanese.

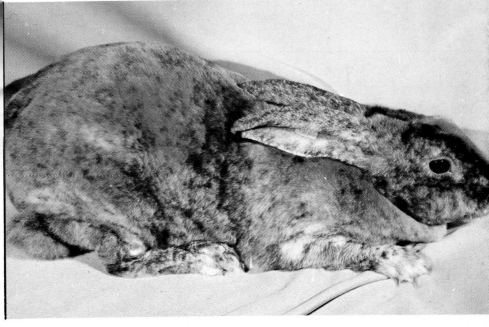

produce in the neighborhood of 90 pounds of edible meat a year.

Rabbits' tremendous reputed capacity for reproduction is no exaggeration. It is estimated that a single pair of rabbits can produce in the neighborhood of 13 million rabbits in three years. An actual case of rabbit over-reproduction occurred in Australia in 1863, when several hundred rabbits escaped from a rabbitry that had been destroyed by fire. Although rabbits were not

An opal agouti Netherland Dwarf rabbit.

A Palomino rabbit.

native to Australia, escaped rabbits became the progenitors of a rabbit population that eventually threatened to overrun much of the continent. These rabbits began eating valuable farm produce and ruining grazing lands. Hunting and trapping did little to stop them, so Australians introduced a viral disease that affected only the rabbits. This restored the balance. Today, Australia is one of the largest producers of rabbits.

Rabbit Fur
Arctic fur, clipped seal, polar seal—these are just some of the names for rabbit fur, which is becoming increasingly popular as some of the more traditional furs disappear. Another newly found use is rabbit wool. Some varieties, like the Angora rabbit, can produce up to twelve ounces per year and, of course, the rabbits do not have to be killed.

The rabbit's coat has three sets of hairs: a dense

A French Lop rabbit with broken color.

A very young albino rabbit with pink eyes. Some white breeds have dark eyes and may even carry other hidden color factors.

underfur, followed by a coarser coat, and finally a long, coarse fur on top. The underfur close to the body is made of fine, short hairs; the top layer is widely distributed and very coarse. The in-between coat conceals the sparseness of the top coat.

Rabbit Varieties

There are more than fifty varieties of rabbits ranging in size from the eleven- to fourteen-pound Flemish Giant to the two- to three-pound Netherland Dwarf. Many of the breeds were first developed for an express purpose, such as meat or pelt production. However, most of the smaller, more modern types were developed solely for exhibition or ornamental purposes, or just for suitability as pets. Let us look at some of the breeds, starting with the older varieties.

Flemish Giant

The Flemish Giant is the largest of all the domestic breeds. An adult can weigh between eleven and fourteen pounds. As it is such a large animal, it should be kept only by those who have space in which to build large hutches and the time and funds to provide great quantities of food. This breed has been popular in the past for both meat and pelt production and is today one of the major exhibition varieties. Fanciers try to breed their specimens as large and as heavy as possible.

The color of the Flemish Giant should be dark gray, finely flecked all over with black. The ears should be large and erect. These rabbits are intelligent and sometimes moody. Most of them, if given plenty of attention, make very affectionate pets.

Belgian Hares

As the name implies, the Belgian Hare is similar in appearance to a hare, in both size and shape. A large, lanky body with long legs and ears make it one of the "racers" of the fancy. Specimens may

Four does: a senior French Lop Broken Madagascar; a senior English Lop tortoiseshell; a senior Mini Lop fawn; and a junior Holland Lop frost point.

The whole family can enjoy the rabbit hobby. Netherland Dwarfs are popular because they are small and are available in many varieties.

Opposite, top: *A Silver Fawn rabbit.* **Opposite, bottom:** *A Silver Rex rabbit.*

weigh up to nine pounds and are normally a beautiful chestnut in color. This breed requires plenty of exercise to keep it trim and should therefore have regular access to outside runs.

English
The English rabbit is one of the more attractive of the fancy breeds. The most popular coloring is black and white, but other colors, including gray and white, chocolate and white, and blue and white are available. The ground is white, and the darker color covers the nose, eyes, and ears, extending into a narrow blotchy line down the spine and appearing as small spots on other parts of the body. It is a medium-size rabbit weighing about seven pounds when adult. It is very hardy and a good breeder, the young growing rapidly. It is very docile and makes an excellent pet.

Himalayan
Another attractive medium-sized rabbit, the Himalayan is usually white with red eyes and black nose, ears, feet and tail, although other colors are occasionally available. It is thought that this variety originated in China. It is a smaller breed than the English, weighing about five pounds, but it is similar in temperament.

Dutch
The Dutch is probably the most widely kept of all the fancy breeds. It is a small, pretty rabbit which has a set of typical markings, a white saddle with rear end and head markings of black, tan, blue, chocolate or gray. Rarely weighing more than five pounds, the Dutch rabbit is a good breeder, and the does are excellent mothers. These rabbits make good all-round pets.

A stunning Black Silver Fox doe.

Both ends of the color range in the self-colored Netherland Dwarf can be seen here—a pink-eyed albino and a pure black.

Opposite, top left: *Each member of the family can have either his or her favorite rabbit.* **Opposite, top right:** *A wild rabbit blends very well in its natural habitat.* **Opposite, bottom:** *A Himalayan Netherland Dwarf rabbit. The standard for this breed requires pink eyes and a pure white body color except for the color markings.*

A six-week-old Blue Fawn English Lop.

English Lop

The Lop is one of the oldest rabbit varieties. It is a heavy rabbit, weighing up to ten pounds, and it has extremely long, wide ears which hang down the side of the head and touch the floor, hence the name "Lop." The usual color is fawn, but fawn and white, black and white, and tortoiseshell and white are occasionally to be seen.

The Lop is not a very active rabbit and does not require a great deal of exercise, but care must be taken that it is not overfed, as it is prone to acquiring fat very quickly. A separate variety is the French Lop, which has shorter ears than the English Lop.

Silver

Another old breed, this medium-size rabbit of five or six pounds in weight is available in three colors: silver-gray, brown, and fawn.

Netherland Dwarf
The smallest of all rabbits, the Netherland Dwarf is a little larger than a guinea pig, and in fact the two animals can be housed together. The Netherland Dwarf comes in almost every color or combination of colors imaginable. An extremely short-eared variety weighing only about two pounds, the breed is very popular as a pet.

Polish
Another small rabbit weighing two to three pounds, the Polish is a white breed which may have blue or red eyes. In spite of its appealing looks,

A Smoke Pearl Netherland Dwarf rabbit.

Water must be available to rabbits at all times, especially during the dry season.

Opposite, top left: *A trio of barn hares enjoying their food. Differences in anatomy and breeding behavior set rabbits and hares apart.* **Opposite, top right:** *A Netherland Dwarf rabbit with some traces of white inherited from its sire.* **Opposite, bottom:** *The correct way of lifting a rabbit. The rear of the animal must be supported as shown.*

it is not an easy breeder and is therefore not recommended for the beginner.

Tan
Black and tan, blue and tan, lilac and tan, and chocolate and tan are the colors available, the tan color being on the underside of the chin and body and also around the rims of the ears. Good specimens have a wonderful sheen to their coats. An adult Tan rabbit weighs about four pounds.

Argente
The Argente varieties originated in France and come in the following colors and sizes. The Argente de Champagne is a blue-haired silver-tipped variety weighing eight or nine pounds. The Argente Bleu is a lavender-haired silver-tipped variety weighing about six pounds. The Argente Creme is a cream-colored rabbit with orange highlights; it

weighs about five pounds. The Argente Brun sports various tones of brown to make up an extremely beautiful coat, the adult rabbit weighing approximately six pounds.

New Zealand
These large rabbits of eight or nine pounds in weight are usually white or brick-red in color. The breed, contrary to its name, is in fact American.

Chinchilla
Originally developed as a fur breed, the Chinchilla has one of the finest coats of all rabbits. The soft gray and blue pelt resembles real chinchilla in both color and texture. These rabbits are docile and make cuddly pets. The Chinchilla rabbit weighs up to six pounds, but a larger

Rabbits are always on the alert during their waking hours, as is shown by this Chinchilla's expression. They are also very inquisitive about their surroundings.

version (called the Chinchilla Giganta) is occasionally available.

Beveren
The Beveren is a large rabbit of seven to eight pounds. It was developed in Belgium as a meat and pelt producer at the turn of the century. It is available in four colors: pure black, pure white, pure brown and pure lavender.

Silver Fox
Named after the fox because its fur is said to resemble a fox's, the Silver Fox rabbit is available in

A New Zealand White rabbit. This breed was developed in America.

An Orange Rex rabbit. Rex rabbits are noted for their short, soft coat.

four color varieties: black, blue, lilac, and chocolate. Each color should be ticked with longer white hairs. An adult Silver Fox weighs between five and seven pounds.

Beaver
A large rabbit, weighing about nine pounds, the Beaver is named after the animal whose coat its own fur resembles.

Rex Rabbit
A Rex rabbit is one in which the stiff guard hairs have been bred out, leaving an extremely short, soft coat which was developed as a valuable pelt breed in the early part of this century. Most of the breeds already described are available in Rex form, the most popular ones being Black, Blue, Lilac, Brown, Chinchilla, Sable,

A Havana rabbit. In this breed, white hairs and white toenails are undesirable in show specimens.

Tan, Himalayan, English, Californian and Dutch.

Californian
This large rabbit is one of the newer breeds. It weighs approximately eight to ten pounds; with its dark ears, feet, nose and tail it looks like a very large Himalayan rabbit.

Havana
This is a medium-size rabbit with a rich chocolate coat having a purplish sheen.

Lilac
This is a medium-size rabbit that should weigh between five and a half and seven pounds. It is

very attractive and has soft pinkish-gray fur.

Sable
These rabbits have very handsome fur coats. They were developed from the Chinchilla breed and weigh between five and seven pounds.

Satin
This rabbit possesses very velvety fur and is available in over twenty different colors. It weighs between six and eight pounds.

Siberian
This British breed was first developed in the 1930's. It

A California rabbit. In this breed, color should be limited to the extremities.

is now available in brown, black, blue and lilac varieties weighing from five to seven pounds.

Smoke Pearl

The coat of this very attractive rabbit, which weighs from five to seven pounds, shades from gray to pearl.

Harlequin

This rabbit is very deserving of its name. Its fur is four very distinct colors arranged in a patchwork. There are different colors on each ear; these colors are reversed in position on the face. The body is covered with distinct rings, and each front foot is a different color, with those colors reversed on the hind feet. This is a very difficult variety to breed and requires true dedication.

Angora

There are many other breeds of rabbit, and it is impossible to describe them all in a volume of this size. There is, however, one breed which deserves special attention—the Angora. This is one of the strangest but most beautiful phenomena in the rabbit world. A well kept Angora has one of the finest and softest coats one can imagine. This coat will require much more attention than that of any other rabbit and must be thoroughly groomed at least once a month to keep the wool from becoming matted and knotted.

Angoras are still kept commercially in many parts of the world and garments manufactured from Angora wool are much sought after and usually expensive. The wool-yielding rabbits are often kept singly in small hutches with a wire floor to prevent the droppings from soiling the coat. The rabbits are sheared about four times a year and a good animal will supply

An albino Angora rabbit. Angora rabbits are especially valued for their fur.

about 12 ounces of wool per annum. The most popular color variety is white, but they do come in other colors, including Chinchilla, Golden, and Smoky.

A pet Angora rabbit can be kept in a smaller hutch than many of the other varieties because, although it is a fairly large breed weighing six to eight pounds, it is rather inactive and spends hours sitting in one position. It is very easy to overfeed an Angora, and they soon put on large quantities of fat if one is not careful. It is advisable to supply Angoras with more green food than other breeds, as this helps keep their long wool in prime condition.

Pet Angoras should be clipped at least once a year, preferably in the summer months, or else a partial molting will occur and not only cause intense matting of the fur but also be extremely irritating to the rabbit. Often this results in a general deterioration in health, followed by sickness caused by the rabbit's pulling out its own coat and eating it. Before clipping, the animal should be thoroughly groomed with a comb or brush and a part made on the line of the spinal ridge. Sharp hairdressing scissors may be used; the wool should be clipped to within half an inch of the skin, but not closer. It is best for two people to perform the operation, one to hold the rabbit and the other to clip it. When clipping the belly of a doe, particularly a pregnant doe, one should keep a sharp watch for the teats, which could be clipped accidentally.

Pet Angora rabbits should be clipped once a year to prevent their fur from matting.

Housing

Most rabbits are extremely hardy and will live without heat through the coldest of winters if they are provided with draft-free and waterproof quarters, dry bedding and a balanced diet.

Keeping hutches in exterior quarters has both advantages and disadvantages. Let us look at the advantages first. If several hutches are to be kept it may be best to keep them in a well lighted shed or garage to reduce the risk of drafts during the winter months. Hutches kept under cover need not be as substantial or as ornamental as those constructed for outdoor use, so they will be cheaper to build. Another advantage of keeping hutches indoors is that the rabbits may be bred at all times of the year, with a minimum loss of young resulting from inclement weather. Finally, it is more pleasant to do the cleaning chores under cover, and therefore the keeper will be less likely to postpone such tasks.

The disadvantages of keeping rabbit hutches under cover are few. Infections may spread extremely quickly in stuffy unventilated buildings, especially where large numbers of animals are kept, but with the provision of ventilating windows positioned so that drafts cannot blow directly into the hutches the risk will be minimized. Rabbits kept in outside hutches which are well protected from the weather are usually the healthiest. They develop thick, sleek coats and are less likely to become infected with airborne germs.

The rabbit fancier therefore has a choice of where to keep his rabbits, and it is entirely up to the individual. Both methods can be satisfactory as long as a few simple rules are followed.

There are many types of

A Dwarf rabbit. No matter how lovely a rabbit looks in a natural setting, it must be provided with adequate shelter, especially during the long winter months.

hutches that can be used for rabbits, and here again it is up to the individual as to what type of hutch to choose. If the rabbits are to be kept indoors, the metal-framed, wire-covered, laboratory type cages may be used. These cages are rather characterless and provide little security for the animals; additionally, these cages are totally unsuitable for breeding.

Earlier authors have recommended orange crates, etc., to be converted into rabbit hutches, but a satisfactory

There are many types of rabbit housing available to the pet owner. Pet shops sell rabbit cages which can be kept indoors.

An English Spot rabbit.

hutch can not be constructed from an orange crate or any other type of fruit box, although the planks from stout crates may be utilized in hutch construction. Fruit crates are usually made from cheap, thin timber and are almost certainly not draft-proof. Attempts at converting such crates into suitable hutches often result in splitting the wood in many places; they result in a most untidy finished construction.

Some of the more popular cages will be described in this chapter. Sizes are given for medium-size rabbits such as Dutch, English and Himalayan and may be altered to accommodate larger or smaller breeds or to suit the particular whims of the fancier.

Single Rabbit Hutch

A single rabbit hutch is suitable for a single pet rabbit or for animals from larger breeding colonies which have to be kept separately, such as bucks separated from does.

For an outside hutch the following size is recommended: length 3½ feet, breadth 18 inches, height at front 20 inches, height at rear 18 inches. The most lasting and attractive material for construction is tongue-and-groove cedarwood boarding mounted on 1¼-inch by 1¼-inch soft timber framing, but to economize, the back, floor, and roof may be made from half-inch plywood.

To construct a plywood hutch, first construct the front and rear frames from 1¼ x 1¼" softwood batten. Any simple type of corner joint will do, but each should be glued and screwed. The outside measurements of the front frame are 3½ by 20 inches; those of the rear frame are 3½ feet by 18 inches. The front frame is provided with a partition stay about one third of the way along its length. The next step is to cut the plywood. Exterior or marine plywood is best if the hutches are to be kept outside, but ordinary ply will do if the hutches are to be kept under cover. Cut the two ends which are 20 inches high in front, 18 inches high at the back and 18 inches in width. Then cut the partition which will be just over 1½ shorter because it is to be fitted over the floor. The top of the partition should have 1¼ x 1¼" slots cut out of its corners to enable it to be fitted into the upper frame. Likewise the floor which is 3½ feet x 18 inches should also have 1¼ x 1¼" slots cut into each corner to take the frame uprights, as well as a further slot to take the front partition stay. The doors should be made

Good housing and a balanced diet go a long way in keeping your pet rabbit healthy and beautiful.

after the main hutch has been assembled so that they can be built to the exact size to allow for mistakes or warping, which may make a slight difference in the frame sizes.

To assemble the hutch, hold the front and rear frames in their approximate positions and nail the floor firmly into place on top of the frame base battens. Next, nail the two ends onto the outside of the frame and fix the partition, with its appropriately sized bolt hole, in the correct position. The partition may be nailed to one side of the partition stay and also carefully through the floor from below. Alternatively, with a little extra work the partition can be made to slide in and out to facilitate easier cleaning. The back is then nailed onto the rear of the frame; if the partition is to be a fixture, the back is nailed onto this as well. The roof, which should overhang the walls of the hutch at least two inches on every side, is then nailed firmly down on to the frame and the ends.

To prepare the wire-fronted door for the main part of the hutch, carefully measure around the area in which it is to fit and then construct a frame to the exact size $1\frac{1}{4}$ x 14″ lumber. Wire mesh of one-inch gauge can be used to cover this, and it generally gives a more attractive appearance if stapled to the inside of the frame. The finished door should be attached by two hinges to the top part of the hutch frame, as this enables the door to be propped up to facilitate easier cleaning. It may be necessary to attach a small piece of

batten to the floor at each end to stop the door from being pushed too far in. A revolving button or a hasp and staple may be used to secure the door at the base.

The door to the rabbit's "bedroom" should be constructed from a solid piece of ply or tongue-and-groove boarding. This again should be cut to fit, and if it is an outside hutch it should be made to overlap so that drafts and rain cannot blow directly into the sleeping quarters.

Finally, for an outside hutch the roof must be covered with a good grade of roofing felt which should be folded down over the edges of the roof and attached from the underside. Quite often it is

Netherland Dwarf rabbits.

possible to continue the felt from the roof right down the back of the hutch to give added protection.

The siting of an outside hutch is important. It should be placed on a stand at least 2 feet from the ground to discourage rats and mice from nesting underneath it, a situation which is certainly not desirable, as these rodents carry diseases. The hutch should be placed in a sheltered position but one in which the sun can shine into the open part of it for at least some of the day. Even rabbits like to sunbathe, and there is evidence that sunlight does them some good.

During severe weather, particularly at night, the front of the hutch can be covered with heavy burlap, attached by four nails to the top of the hutch and a couple of cup hooks at the bottom. The burlap can be unhooked at the bottom and folded over the top of the cage during the day.

Breeding Hutches
A breeding hutch should be similar in design to the single rabbit hutch but a little larger and with a few modifications. A good size for a breeding hutch for medium-size rabbits would be 47 inches long by 23 inches deep by 22 inches high at the front and 20 inches at the back. One third of it should again be used as nesting quarters; a removable safety plank 4 inches wide is placed at the bottom of this, just inside the door. This helps to stop the bedding and also young rabbits from falling out when the door is opened.

To prevent mother rabbit from being over-suckled by her youngsters it is advisable to fit a rest platform for her about 8

A mother and baby rabbit. Breeding hutches should provide a place for the mother rabbit to take a break from her young.

inches from the base of the hutch. The platform can be about 6 inches wide for a medium-size doe. She can get up onto it out of the way if she needs a rest from the litter.

If several breeding females are to be kept, a battery of breeding hutches containing three to six units may be constructed. A frame is made to take the required size and number of hutches, preferably from stout lumber approximately 2 inches x 3 inches. More than three tiers of hutches are not recommended, as servicing would then become too difficult.

There is no end to the variety of hutches one can construct, and this is one of the joys of rabbit keeping, especially if one is a keen carpenter.

The Morant Hutch

A popular type of rabbit hutch is one in which rabbits can graze directly from a lawn or other grassy patch. The Morant hutch, invented by Major G. Morant towards the end of the last century, is one such construction. It consists basically of a triangular arc, two thirds of which is covered with wire netting, the remaining third being a covered house. The whole of the floor is also covered with wire netting to stop the rabbits from burrowing out but enabling them to graze from the grass upon which the hutch is resting. To prevent fouling of any particular area the hutch should be moved daily to a new patch.

Although this type of hutch is normally in use during the warmer parts of the year, it does help to cut down on the food bill, gives the animals more interest in being able to forage for their own food and certainly helps to improve the health of the inhabitants.

A good-sized Morant

A three-week-old Blue Silver Fox rabbit.

hutch is about 59 inches in length and 32 inches high at the apex. The house should take up 20 inches of the length and should be covered with tongue-and-groove boarding. Inside the house a raised shelf should be fitted to enable the rabbits to sleep on a dry surface should they wish. As this type of hutch is meant to be easily transportable, it should not be made too heavy. The framework should be constructed of fairly light battens, 1¼ x 1¼″. The easiest way to make a Morant hutch is to use small triangular pieces of plywood. However, a neater frame is produced when one takes the trouble to join it properly.

The Colony Pen

One of the most interesting ways of keeping rabbits, if one has the space, is the colony system of allowing one buck to run with several does in a large open-air pen, something similar to a chicken run. The ambitious fancier can construct something quite elaborate and ornamental; shrubs and creepers can be grown in strategic positions around the pen, and the weather-proof nesting quarters can be built to resemble an Alpine villa or even a Chinese pagoda. The house should be set on a concrete base and separate nesting boxes should be placed inside for the buck and each doe. In very bad weather the animals can be locked into the house. Care should be taken in the construction of the house to see that all parts are easily accessible for cleaning purposes and that no superfluous niches are left for the benefit of mice or rats.

The outer pen should have a wire netting wall about 6½ feet high, the top foot of which should be angled out to prevent the entry of cats and other predators. The base of the wire should be bent inwards for about 2 feet to prevent the rabbits from burrowing out. Once the initial grass has been destroyed by the rabbits the floor of the pen can be covered with sand, which may be replaced as necessary.

The size of the run depends on the number of rabbits to be kept and the amount of available space, but as a general guideline a pen 13 feet by 6½ feet should be adequate for one buck and eight does.

A black Netherland Dwarf rabbit.

Although it is very nice to possess a single cuddly pet rabbit, one cannot achieve complete satisfaction in rabbit-keeping until one has attempted breeding. What can be more exciting than the inspection of a first litter or seeing the young rabbits emerge from their nursery for the first time?

Rabbits are not difficult to breed, in fact they are quite prolific, hence the saying "they breed like rabbits." A female, or doe, reaches sexual maturity in four to eight months, depending usually upon the size of the variety. A Netherland Dwarf, for instance, will be mature in four months, whereas a Flemish Giant will be seven or eight months old before she is ready for mating.

How does one sex a rabbit? In adults this is relatively easy, as the male has a very prominent scrotum which is not present on the doe. In younger rabbits this is much more difficult, because the scrotum takes some time to become fully developed. It is advisable for two people to be present for sexing, one to restrain the rabbit and the other to manipulate the genitalia. One person should hold the rabbit's belly upwards, preferably on a flat surface, with its hindlegs spread apart. The other person applies pressure to either side of the vent until either the penis of the buck or the vagina of the doe is evident. This can be ascertained by size, a penis being longer than the corresponding organ in the female. Also, the female organ has a much larger aperture.

Before breeding a pair of rabbits it is wise to

A pair of Lop rabbits. One of the most exciting aspects of breeding is seeing the different colors of the newly arrived young.

An English Spot rabbit. Breeding rabbits which conform to a particular standard is one of the challenges rabbit keepers enjoy most.

ascertain a few facts. For instance, are they really a true pair? Are they of the right breed? Are they in breeding condition?

Selection of the correct breed is of great importance. If one is breeding exhibition specimens, the good points of each member of the pair are the prime consideration. Pairings to produce exhibition rabbits are usually either the best doe in a stud paired with the best buck, or else individuals chosen in hopes that the outstanding features of each rabbit in the pair will balance out the slight failings of the other rabbit. There is always an element of chance when breeding, and this uncertainty adds to the excitement for most breeders. From experience a breeder will soon learn which rabbits tend to pass their outstanding traits on to their offspring and which individuals, although of very good quality themselves, do not produce quality offspring.

Accurate and complete records should be kept as a basis on which the breeder can make decisions for pairing. These records should include details of the parent rabbits, the birth

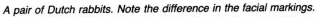

A pair of Dutch rabbits. Note the difference in the facial markings.

date of the litter and the show history of each offspring. After a few generations have been bred the breeder will have an invaluable source of information.

In order to bring a newly purchased pair of rabbits into breeding condition it is wise to keep them separate for about two weeks, during which time they are fed a good balanced diet. If the rabbits are mature there should be no problem in achieving a quick mating. Unlike most other groups of mammals, lagomorphs do not come "in heat" only at specific periods but may

A recently kindled litter of rabbit pups. Rabbits are born naked and blind.

A Florida white buck and a Chocolate Pan buck rabbit.

be induced to do so by a mating gesture from the buck at almost any time of the year, although most prolifically in the months from February to September.

It is normally the practice to take the doe to the buck's hutch, because a buck is much more likely to perform successfully when he is on his own territory. Mating in rabbits is extremely fast, so do not be unduly worried if the buck seems to fall off the doe after only a few seconds, for this can quite often have been a successful mating.

After mating, the doe is returned to the breeding hutch. There will be a covered area where the doe can build her nest and bear her young. Do not forget the platform onto which the doe can jump in times of stress when her litter becomes too overbearing for her.

Some breeders like to supply the pregnant doe with a nest box as well as an enclosed compartment. In hutches with no enclosed compartment a nest box is essential, as the litter must be protected from drafts. A nest box can be made

A Blue Beveren rabbit.

A trio of rabbits. No mother rabbit should be expected to care for too many pups.

from plywood or planking and will vary in accordance with the size of the breed, but an average-size rabbit such as an English will make do with a box some 16 inches long by 10 inches wide by 6 inches deep. One of the short sides of the box should have a hole cut into it to allow the doe to enter and leave the box easily. Holes should be drilled in the base of the box and two slats nailed under the base so that it does not rest directly on the floor of the hutch, thus allowing for ventilation and keeping the box dry.

Occasionally a doe will

build a nest outside the nest box or even in the open part of the hutch. In this case it is wise to put the nest that she has built into the box and position the box over the space where she had built the nest herself. If the doe still insists on building her nest elsewhere it is advisable to keep the hutch partially shielded with sacking and leave her where she is.

The average gestation for a rabbit is 31 days. The average of course varies upwards and downwards with individual animals. It is often difficult to tell whether a doe is pregnant, or "in kindle" as the

A family of Castor Rex rabbits—buck, doe, and litter.

A Golden Dutch rabbit, an unusual and beautiful variety.

fanciers call it, until the latter part of the pregnancy.

One method that has been suggested is that if the mated doe is reintroduced to a buck about two days after the initial mating, the female will violently repel any advances from the male if she is genuinely in kindle. This method is, however, never 100% foolproof. During the latter part of the pregnancy it is fairly easy to ascertain by palpation whether the doe is in kindle. Palpation is the gentle feeling of the doe's abdomen with the fingertips with the object

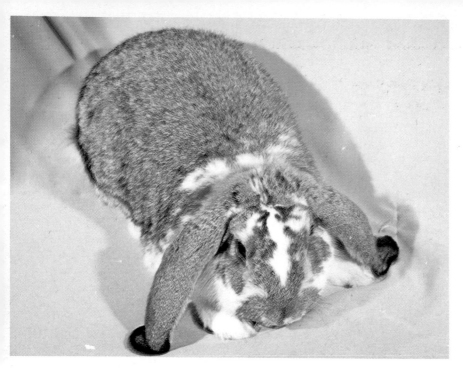

Above: *A French Lop rabbit.* **Below:** *A Dwarf Lop rabbit.* **Opposite, top left:** *An Argente Creme rabbit.* **Opposite, top right:** *This small Himalayan rabbit is four months old and will soon be fully grown.* **Opposite, bottom:** *A portable cage is adequate for a small breed of rabbits. It can be carried anywhere and placed where conditions are ideal.*

of detecting the presence of embryonic young. With practice this becomes very easy, but take heed—too rough handling of the doe during this period will result in the loss of the litter. During the latter part of the pregnancy the doe should be disturbed as

little as possible. This will enforce her feeling of security and result in her being more likely to be a good mother when the time comes.

Be sure that the doe has an ample supply of nesting materials. Straw, hay, or wood shavings make a

A Broken Fawn Holland Lop, age three months.

Before breeding any rabbit, be sure it is in good health and is physically mature enough to handle the responsibility of caring for a litter.

good base, and the doe will line the inside of the nest with fur plucked from her own underside.

Do not be unduly worried if shortly before kindling time the doe goes off her food or if her droppings become soft.

This is normal and will right itself after the young have been born. At kindling time the doe will require much more water than usual, so it is a good idea to check the water dish two or three times a day. A thirsty doe is likely

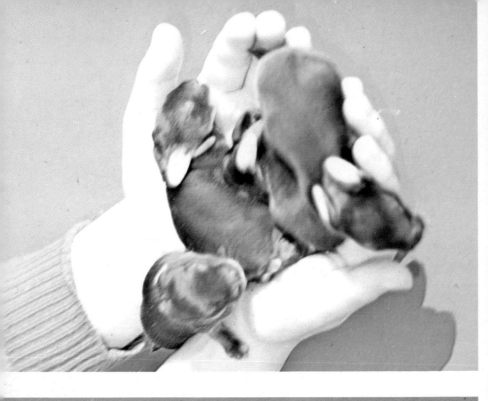

Most commercial breeders separate the litter as early as possible to allow the doe to rest and get fattened for the next breeding.

Opposite, top: *At four days, these Black and Tan rabbits are so small that four of them can fit into two hands.* **Opposite, bottom:** *A much larger Black and Tan rabbit at the age of eleven days.*

A blue-eyed white Netherland Dwarf rabbit.

to kill and eat her litter, so make sure this unfortunate result does not occur. An increase in greenfood during the pregnancy is also advised as well as extra root crops such as carrots, all of which go towards helping the doe produce a good supply of milk for her young. In fact, it is not a bad idea to give the doe a dish of diluted milk once a day in lieu of water. These measures can be continued during the nursing period until shortly before weaning.

When it is noticed that a doe is about to kindle it is wise to leave her undisturbed until at least twenty-four hours after the birth. If the nest is then looked at, slight movements in the nesting material will indicate that the birth has taken place, as will the slimmer appearance of the mother rabbit.

It is advisable to examine the litter as soon as possible after this

A standard Himalayan rabbit.

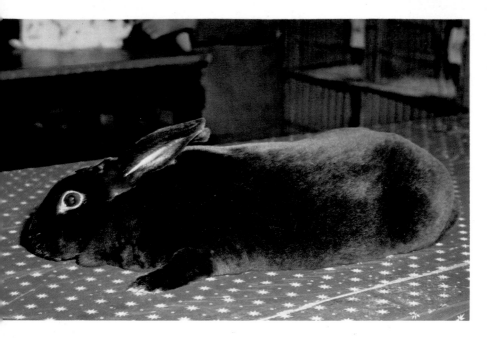

Above: *A Black Rex rabbit.* **Below:** *An Orange Rex rabbit.*

Above: *A New Zealand Red rabbit.* **Below:** *An Orange Rex rabbit with an identification tag in its ear.*

twenty-four hour period has elapsed to ascertain that all has gone well. Gently remove the doe from the hutch and give her some special tidbit to keep her mind occupied while the nest is being examined. Before touching the nest the hands should be rubbed in the floor litter to remove the human smell which might upset the doe. Baby rabbits are totally blind and almost naked at birth. Their ears are remarkably small and, in fact, the babies do not look like little rabbits at all. It is often difficult to convince onlookers that litters of baby rabbits are in fact rabbits and not rats or guinea pigs. The

A tortoiseshell Dutch rabbit.

A trio of English Lops: a broken blue, a lynx, and a broken opal.

comparative nakedness of baby rabbits, by the way, is one of the things that differentiates rabbits from hares. Newborn hares are not naked; they are covered with fur, and they are ready to start running around within a few hours of being born, which is definitely not true of newborn rabbits.

Any dead babies should be removed at once, and the remainder can be quickly examined. It is possible to sex them when they are still without fur by

At most, a Netherland Dwarf can weigh about two and a half pounds according to the standard of the breed.

Opposite, left: *A Fawn rabbit.* **Opposite, right:** *A Dutch rabbit.* **Opposite, bottom:** *A Marten Sable Netherland Dwarf rabbit.*

A Lilac Mini Lop rabbit.

the presence of small white spots which indicate the teats in does. After the fur has grown this is no longer possible, in which case the more conventional method of identification must be used.

Any obvious runts should also be removed and humanely destroyed. Also, if the litter is excessively large it may be necessary to remove one or more. It is better to have fewer rabbits in good condition than a litter of twelve deformed runts. Six is the maximum number a doe should be allowed to raise herself. Any in excess of this number can be destroyed, fostered or hand-reared.

Fostering is sometimes possible when two does are in kindle at the same time; one may have a litter of eight and the other a litter of four, for instance. In this case two would be taken from the doe with the large litter and given to the other, thus limiting the litters to six each.

Fostering should be done as soon as possible after the birth, up until three days of age. Fosterings after this time are usually risky but may occasionally be successful. The safest time for redistributing the litters is definitely when the young are about a day old.

As when examining the nest, the does should be

A Black Dutch rabbit. An average Dutch rabbit grows to about five pounds.

Above: *A Chinchilla rabbit, two years old.* **Below:** *A Siamese Sable rabbit.*

Above: *A Chinchilla Rex rabbit.* **Below:** *A Silver Gray rabbit.*

A pair of Black Dutch rabbits. Young rabbits should not be removed from the nest until they are old enough to be away from their mother.

removed and given some tasty tidbits to occupy their minds while the change around is being carried out. Rub your hands in hutch litter and pick up the young from the large litter which are to be fostered and place them into the new nest. If there is some distance from one hutch to the other, it is best to carry the young in a box lined with some warm, soft material; young rabbits can chill very quickly if left out in the cold for very long.

Once the initial examination of the litter has been completed and any necessary changes carried out, the doe should be left to rear the young on her own and should be disturbed as little as possible. What can be a better parent than the genuine mother of the infant? However, it may sometimes be necessary to rear young rabbits by hand as described later.

The doe will do all that is necessary to keep her new litter in good health. She will keep the nest at the right temperature by adding or removing material as the weather changes, and it is therefore wise to see that a little extra nesting material is always available, particularly during cold weather. She will feed her young from her own milk supply at regular intervals. The young know how to find the teats by instinct and will eagerly attach themselves and drink their fill. She will keep the nest clean by removing soiled

A pair of Blue and Tan rabbits.

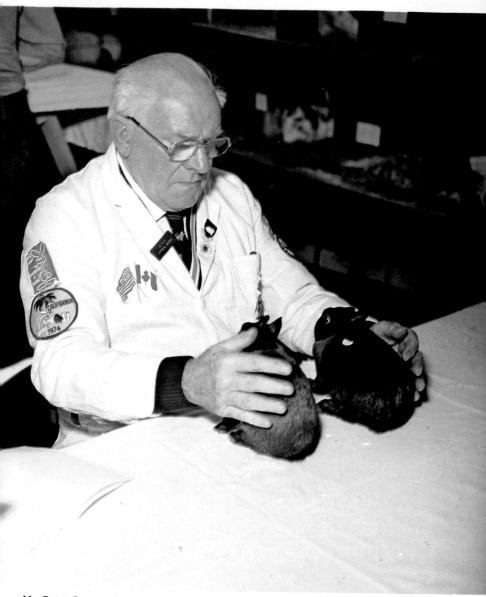

Mr. Peter Cage of England is seen here judging a pair of Netherland Dwarf rabbits.

Opposite: An English Lop rabbit with a broken color pattern.

A litter of mixed pups. Note the variations in their coat patterns.

material and replacing it with fresh, so ensure that the run part of the hutch is kept clean.

As the youngsters feed steadily they will grow plump and their fur will develop rapidly. Their eyes will open after about ten days and within three weeks they should be leaving the nest and running about the hutch floor. If the young leave the nest before they are three weeks old it could mean that the doe is not supplying them with

A Black Silver Marten rabbit.

Above: *Rabbits come in all sizes, colors, markings, and with different lengths and textures of hair.* **Left:** *A Marten Sable Polish rabbit.* **Opposite, left:** *The Polish is a small breed, but is not as small as the Netherland Dwarf.* **Opposite, right:** *A Brittania Petite rabbit.* **Opposite, below:** *A Havana Rex rabbit. Its rich, chocolate brown coloration is reminiscent of the famous Havana cigars.*

enough milk, so make sure that she is getting a good supply of water and greenfood in particular. The greenfood will enrich the mother's milk passed onto the youngsters, thus preparing them for their first solid meals when they leave the nest.

Usually the first time that the young rabbits can be thoroughly examined is when they have just left the nest. They must be checked for any abnormalities. One of the most common defects in rabbits of this age is bad eyes, often caused by the eyes' failing to open properly after being infected by bacteria. They may be bathed in water in which a few boric acid crystals have been dissolved. A good veterinary eye ointment then applied should cure this complaint completely.

The first few weeks of a rabbit's life are the critical ones, because it is some time before the youngster can build up immunities to help it fight off disease. Therefore, hygiene at this stage is of the utmost importance; hutches should be kept spotless in spite of the fact that they become dirtier more quickly with a large litter running about in them. Food should be regular and clean, and any sudden changes must be avoided. As the youngsters grow, the quantity will increase until they gradually want more to eat than adult rabbits. They must have ample food supplies if they are to grow naturally.

When the young are between six and seven weeks old they can be separated from the doe. So that the emotional strain is not too great all at once, it is best to remove the doe from the litter rather than the litter from the doe. This allows the youngsters to adjust to being without their mother before being moved into strange surroundings.

A Black Fox rabbit being judged according to the breed standard.

They can be left in the nursery hutch for a further few days before being placed in stock hutches. If one is going to sell the youngsters, now is probably the best time to do so.

Once the young have been sorted out it is time to have a look at the doe. See that she is in a dry, comfortable hutch. Examine her for any sign of ill health and feed her well. Above all, let her rest for at least three weeks after weaning off her litter

A lovely family of Dutch rabbits. One of the joys of rabbit keeping lies in the fact that the experience is enjoyable for the young and old alike.

before attempting to mate her again, waiting even longer if she is not 100% after this time.

Rabbits are capable of producing several litters of young each year, but it is not advisable to allow a doe more than three if she is to remain in top form. There are records of commercially kept does producing up to eleven litters in one season, but in

A Smoke Pearl Brittania Petite rabbit.

A pair of rabbits going for a "ride."

such cases the young are usually fostered. Where a particular doe is superb, fostering of course is one method of producing more young in a shorter period without causing much strain on the parent.

A phenomenon which occasionally occurs among rabbits is pseudopregnancy: a doe will carry out all the usual nesting activities but will not produce youngsters, as the mating with the buck was for some reason or other not productive. If nothing else, pseudo pregnancies indicate that a doe is ready for mating, and an animal in this condition when introduced to a buck is most likely to conceive.

The length of time a mother rabbit can be kept as a breeder may vary from variety to variety or even from individual to

One must be careful not to overbreed a rabbit; otherwise, its health may suffer. It is the raising of the young that is stressful to the rabbit.

The hand-reared rabbit makes a gentler pet, since it has lost all fear of its human owner.

individual, but three years is an average breeding life. The average over-all life span in domestic rabbits is probably in the region of five years, but records of twelve years or more are known, especially in does which have not been used for breeding.

The buck rabbit may be used to serve a doe as soon as he is mature. If he is receiving a balanced diet and is fit and is not overweight, he is capable of mating almost daily. This is not usually necessary unless the fancier is producing extremely large numbers of youngsters. The best stud bucks are those which are kept well away from the does and introduced to them for mating at intervals of about fourteen days. Mating then usually takes place in a very short time, often in a matter of seconds.

Occasionally, in cases of the mother rabbit's death or during severe sickness, the litter may have to be hand-reared. This is something which takes a lot of time and a great deal of patience, but the results are often very rewarding. A hand-reared youngster always makes a much better pet than a mother-reared one, because it loses all fear of its human foster parent. The orphan should be fed at three-hour intervals with a good milk mixture. A commercial baby milk is ideal, and this should be mixed at about one and a half times the strength recommended for newborn babies. Rabbit milk is highly concentrated compared to that of most other domestic animals, so the young must have a highly concentrated artificial food. The milk may be given from an eye dropper or even from a toy doll's feeding bottle, and pet shops sell nursing bottles designed for use in feeding orphaned baby animals. The size of the aperture is really something which must be worked out by trial and error. In other words, one must try and establish how much milk the rabbit is going to drink in a certain amount of time without causing any discomfort to the animal.

Once the correct quantity and concentration of the artificial food has been discovered, the baby rabbits should develop at a similar rate as those which are reared by their mothers. By the age of three weeks the youngsters should be encouraged to eat solid foods and to drink from a

A Chocolate Silver Fox rabbit.

dish. As soon as they start feeding themselves the "bottle" feeds can be gradually decreased until they are no longer required, just as with a human baby—but fortunately weaning a rabbit does not take quite the same length of time.

Rabbits are herbivorous animals; therefore, one must be sure that pet rabbits do not have access to any poisonous plants.

valuable source of energy and warmth. Additionally, care should be used in the selection of grains to feed, for not all contain fiber, which is necessary for good digestion. Luckily for rabbit owners, commercially prepared rabbit pellets ensure that a proper mixture of vitamins is given. Rabbit pellets can be purchased at any pet shop, and it is highly recommended that they be used as the principal source of diet. Most rabbit keepers feed rabbit pellets twice daily, with a mixture of hay and oats. Once weekly a supply of leafy greens and roots are given.

Care of the Doe and Her Litter

For the pregnant doe an

Rabbits need a more specialized diet than is usually supposed. Their principal food needs are ash or minerals, fats, proteins and fiber. Since rabbits are herbivorous and eat no meats, their diet is limited in fats, a

A balanced diet is a must for a healthy pet rabbit. Variety will help keep the rabbit interested in its food and will increase the likelihood that it is receiving adequate nutrition.

ample supply of rabbit pellets should be provided at all time. There is no danger of the doe's overfeeding at such time. Milk should be provided and whole oats, if possible, the highly nutritious oats used for racehorses. Oats and other grains are valuable sources of protein and carbohydrates. Carbohydrates contain starches and sugars that are necessary for energy and heat. Since the rabbit eats little natural fat, it must make up for this deficiency by ingesting vast quantities of carbohydrates. For the newborn litter they should

The results of a good diet are a beautiful coat and clear, sparkling eyes.

Since rabbits do not eat meat, they must be given foods which contain sufficient amounts of protein and carbohydrates.

be fed more oats than rabbit pellets, which are a little too hard for them to chew.

Water

Since rabbits are fed dry foods, water is all-important. A heavy bowl— one that the rabbits will not tip over—should be used, or one that is firmly rooted to the cage floor. The rabbits should not go a day without an adequate supply of water. The water **must** be clean and fresh.

Perhaps the best watering device is a water dripper. This is an inverted

A senior doe French Lop, and a senior buck Holland Lop. Note the difference in their sizes.

glass bottle with a metal tube attached. These water drippers work on a gravity principle; the animal sucks or licks water from the tube, and the water that is consumed is displaced at the top of the

Facing: *A rabbit feeding in the wild. The diet of the pet rabbit must provide the nutrients the wild rabbit can find in its natural habitat.*

glass bottle by air bubbles. No air actually enters the glass from outside. Check with your local pet dealer on the size to be used. Too small a tube will not deliver enough water, and too large a hole will also cause trouble.

Supplementary Food
The following is a breakdown of the nutrition content required by an adult rabbit. The foods that follow each entry will supply the nutrient content required but should be used only as a supplement to the basic diet of rabbit

pellets. It is important not to overfeed new rabbits and to remember that sudden dietary changes may cause diarrhea.

Sources of dry roughage include alfalfa hay, peanut hay, soybeans and oat hay.

Sources of greens are carrots, sweet potatoes and turnips. Be sure to feed the roots also.

Commonly fed grains for carbohydrates and protein are barley, beet pulp, bread, buckwheat, corn, milk, oats, peanut meal and wheat. Some of these foods will have to be ground before serving.

If one gives the pet rabbit a well-balanced diet, the rabbit should live a long, healthy life.

An important part of the health of a rabbit is its environment. A clean cage or hutch is imperative to the health of the rabbit.

Fortunately, rabbits are basically sturdy animals. If kept in a clean, well-kept rabbitry, they should live out their lives without their owner's having to worry about their contracting any diseases. Yearly visits to the veterinarian for a health checkup will help nip any latent diseases that might be infecting a hutch of rabbits, but, generally speaking, worms, mites, and pneumonia can all be controlled by keeping clean, dry hutches. An all-wire cage is the best insurance for maintaining a clean rabbitry.

Facing:
A healthy rabbit is a happy rabbit and a beautiful rabbit, just like the one shown.

In an all-wire cage the urine and manure pass right through to a pit below. The rabbits' feet stay clean in this way, which in itself is a major preventive of ringworm and tapeworm. Also, the wire has to be cleaned only once a week with a wire brush. Odors will be kept to a minimum, which will keep away flies.

The hay or shavings should be cleaned at least once a month, or when they become dried out. The only exception to this is during mating, when disturbing the doe might

The best way to ensure a healthy adult rabbit is to see that, as a baby, it has a good start in life.

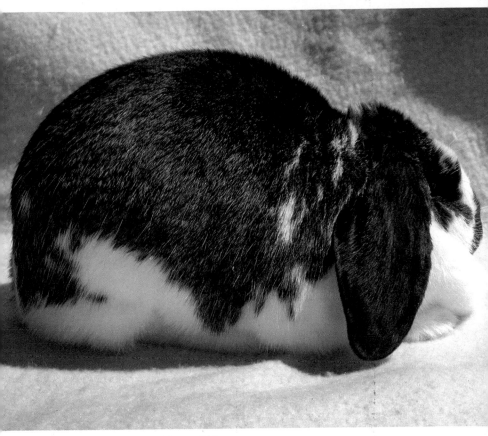

A Broken Steel French Lop rabbit.

lead to cannibalism or stillbirths.

The rest of this chapter will be devoted to some of the common health rules as regards the keeping of rabbits, plus some of the diseases and cures. Should a rabbit become sick it should always be

A six-month-old Holland Lop buck rabbit.

taken to a vet.

Molt
The first molt occurs sometime between a rabbit's sixth and fifteenth week. Do not mistake this normal fur-shedding for the shedding caused by ticks or fur disease. Molt has been mistaken for mucoid enteritis, which is a great killer of young rabbits.

For the young molting rabbits, some linseed or cod liver oil should be added to the diet to replace natural oils. Add about one-half teaspoon to

A Siamese Smoke Pearl Netherland Dwarf rabbit.

A rabbit should go to the veterinarian regularly, as should all other pets.

the daily diet.

Mucoid Enteritis

Mucoid enteritis is a form of diarrhea that strikes young rabbits between five to eight weeks of age. This is a very fast killer, often taking less than 24 hours. Symptoms include a change in behavior: the rabbit begins sitting listlessly in a corner, sometimes with his feet in the water crock because of fever; the feces are jellylike and will soil the rabbit's underside; because the rabbit can not maintain its food, its fur becomes scruffy, and the rabbit itself looks squint-eyed and thin, with mucus around the mouth. Another way to detect mucoid enteritis is to pick the rabbit up and shake him. A splashing sound can be heard within.

The rabbit should be taken to a veterinarian for treatment. He can

A Dutch Brown-Gray rabbit.

A Blue Silver Fox doe rabbit.

prescribe medication to combat this disease, which once was thought to be incurable.

Heat Exhaustion

Heat exhaustion can occur if the rabbits are left under the direct glare of the sun during a hot day. The rabbits can succumb in a matter of hours. Symptoms include lying on the side and breathing heavily. Since this is basically a case of negligence, it is more easy to prevent than to cure.

The best preventive measure is to provide lots

of water and to set up a salt block inside the hutch in hot, humid weather. Some form of shade should be provided if the cage cannot be moved, such as using a tarpaulin during the mid-day.

To treat a rabbit suffering from heat exhaustion, immerse it in a bucket of luke warm (not cold, or the rabbit may go into shock) water. Also, when immersing the rabbit, keep its head bare.

Pasteurellosis
This is a non-lethal disease that is characterized by sneezing and coughing. It is sometimes simply called "runny" nose, for it is very much like that. The rabbit emits a thin, runny substance from its nose

The rabbit which is kept outdoors must be provided with shelter from the sun. If it is not, the rabbit may fall victim to heat exhaustion.

*A one-month-old
Chocolate Holland Lop.*

and, using its fur to wipe on, soon gets a caked substance over its fur.

Ear Mites

Ear mites are common and can be difficult to remove. Ear mites can be diagnosed by the formation of crusts in the ears, caused by the rabbit's continually scratching them with its paws. Stiff neck and muscle spasms of the eyes are also symptoms. To clean off the crusts, use hydrogen peroxide. Your veterinarian can give you a medication to swab around the ears and head region.

Another treatment is the use of mineral oil. Crusts

An English Spot rabbit, a member of one of the oldest fancy breeds.

A young Holland Lop rabbit.

treated with this oil will loosen and fall off. This will also help to kill the mites.

Sore Hocks

The condition known as sore hocks is caused by a number of things. One is the chafing of the fur against the wire or wood of the cage, which is unavoidable. Another is the foot-stomping that

rabbits use for signalling. Sometimes the bruises become infected and should be treated. Tincture of iodine or an antibiotic ointment should clear up the condition. When treating, give the rabbit a board to sit on.

Coccidiosis

Coccidiosis is a protozoan disease that affects the liver. Lack of appetite and bloated abdomen are two of the symptoms of this disease.

Affected rabbits should be removed and treated with sulfaquinoxaline mixed in with their food.

A trio of English Lop rabbits.

A lovely Mini Lop rabbit.

Index

RABBITS
KW-021